the little book of cat tricks

the little book of cat tricks

sandra toney   illustrated by kristin doney

HOWELL
BOOK
HOUSE

Copyright © 2003 by Wiley Publishing, Inc., New York, NY

Howell Book House

Published by Wiley Publishing, Inc., New York, NY

For general information on our other products and services or to obtain technical support please contact our Customer Care Department within the U.S. at 800-762-2974, outside the U.S. at 317-572-3993 or fax 317-572-4002.

Wiley also publishes its books in a variety of electronic formats. Some content that appears in print may not be available in electronic books.

Library of Congress Cataloging-in-Publication Data

Toney, Sandra L.
    The little book of cat tricks / Sandra Toney ; illustrated by Kristin Doney.
        p. cm.
    ISBN 978-1-62045-726-9
    1. Cats--Training. I. Title.
    SF446.6 .T66 2002
    636.8'0887--dc21

                                        2002009967

Manufactured in the United States of America
10 9 8 7 6 5 4 3 2 1

Book design by Holly Wittenberg
Cover design by Susan Olinsky and Holly Wittenberg

table of contents

the real trick to training cats

There's a guarded secret that many of our feline friends don't want to let out of the bag. Despite cats' long-standing reputation as aloof creatures, they do like to ham it up, learn new tricks and—yes—even please us. Keep this in mind—you *can* teach tricks to even the most finicky feline.

Like dogs, cats crave our attention and approval. They just may not be as demonstrative of their desires. It's a myth (probably first started by canines) that dogs—and only dogs—are capable of learning commands and tricks. Dogs may thump their tails and paw their chests in the contention that trick performing proves that they are smarter than felines. Not so! Both species have their share of spotlight seekers—natural performers ever so eager to master tricks or commands.

The trick for *you* is in knowing what makes your cat tick. First, it is vital to acknowledge that cats are not small dogs—not in body structure, personality or attitude. If you trace the domestic cat's lineage, you will discover that cats of ancient times were solitary

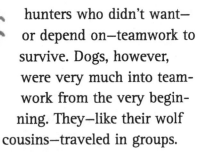 hunters who didn't want—or depend on—teamwork to survive. Dogs, however, were very much into teamwork from the very beginning. They—like their wolf cousins—traveled in groups.

Ancestors of the modern dog recognized that individual survival hinged on cooperation from all members of the pack.

But don't let the history of cats slow you down in your trick-teaching pursuits. Anyone who cares about cats can teach his feline friend a trick or two—or three. You don't have to be a professional trainer, or enroll in a special cat training school, to achieve success. You just need to be consistent, caring and patient. And remember that cats are whizzes at reading our body language, our voice tones and even our emotions.

Make your training sessions more like a game and less like a chore. Bring plenty of enthusiasm and encouragement to these sessions. If you force a trick or become impatient or—worse—demanding, your cat will probably leave the scene in a huff. Also, avoid long training sessions. Cats quickly become bored by chores and may once again stalk off, leaving you holding the bag—of tricks!

The beauty of this book is that both you and your cat come out winners. You will learn how to read your cat's body language and identify those ideal times when your cat is in a receptive mood and you can try a new trick. Tricks ease boredom from your cat's life and instill renewed vigor. Also, by working together as a team, the two of you can form an even tighter friendship bond.

This book covers lots of tricks, from your basic "Sit" (see chapter 2) to the more complex "Gimme Five" greeting (see chapter 17) to the ever-so-cool "Leash Walking" (see chapter 6). And each trick provides fun and easy instructions. Think back to your school days and your very favorite teacher. What made this teacher so special? What did he or she do to motivate you to try your very best? Keep this teacher's approach in mind when you trick train your cat. After all, the very best teachers know how to trigger an enthusiasm and a willingness to learn in their students (two-legged *and* four-legged).

One caveat: In general, teaching tricks to a declawed cat may take some extra research and patience. After all, claws are very important to a cat's balance—both physical and mental.

As with all the tricks in this book, an adult should do the teaching—or at least supervising—of Kitty's tricks. Sometimes youngsters don't express themselves calmly enough for a cat to understand exactly what is going on. And an irritated feline could scratch a child who is just trying to teach her a trick. Kitty's adult owner—or another adult she knows and trusts very well—should teach her most of these tricks. Cats don't necessarily appreciate change in their lives, so when trying to teach them something new, a familiar face behind the training is preferable.

Consistency is the trick that you yourself will need to learn. Cats understand more easily than some may think, but you are the key—you must be consistent in your training techniques or Kitty will be confused if you vary the way you teach her to perform a trick. Your training regularity is a crucial element in the success or failure of feline training.

And remember—train 'em young. Generally, the younger the kitten, the more willing the student.

feline truisms

Before you launch into trick teaching, devote a few days—or even a week—to looking at your cat in a whole new way. Focus a little extra attention on your cat's actions and habits. You may start to notice that your cat chum typically displays many—if not all—of the following characteristics:

Cats are creatures of routine. Cats like to wake up at a certain time (usually 45 minutes *before* your alarm clock chimes), eat at a certain time (again, 45 minutes *before* your alarm clock sounds) and welcome you home at a certain time. If cats were people, they would work on an assembly line on the same shift for their entire career. Cats will quickly learn your daily schedule and adapt accordingly.

Cats detest change and hate confusion. Cats live for consistency, which explains why some cats scamper under the bed when your cigar-smoking Uncle Mack pays a surprise overnight visit. Or why some cats hide deep in the bedroom closet when they see packing boxes stacked in your living room. ("Who could be moving?" they may ponder silently.) Their schedule has been up-ended, and they must find a safe spot where they can regroup.

Cats are true homebodies. Cats feel most comfortable in familiar surroundings. This is another area where cats differ from dogs. Dogs are people-oriented. Dogs are willing to journey with their favorite people to strange new places to take in new sights, sounds and smells. Cats prefer their home turf—it gives them a feeling of having the home-field advantage. Few cats are begging their owners to take them in the car for a ride downtown and a day of shopping.

Cats are supreme snoozers. Call them Rip van Felines because they love to sleep. Insomnia is hardly a common affliction among cats who have mastered the fine art of zzzzzs. When you total all the naps and long snoozes, cats—*on average*—sleep 16 or more hours a day. And they rarely regret missing a day's event. There's always *tomorrow* to hold vigil on the windowsill and watch the birds fly into the feeder that dangles on the oak tree outside. Cats select comfy, cozy places to nap. Some follow the day's sun, moving from room to room;

others like to nap on high perches, such as bookshelves, while others will burrow deep under the bedspread for an afternoon siesta.

Cats are completely candid. Cats never lie or pretend or sugarcoat. If they don't want to sit on your lap, they will make like Houdini— wiggle free and disappear. It's nothing personal, mind you. They would just rather be elsewhere. But if a cat desires some TLC from y-o-u, she will stroll over without hesitation, plop on your lap and flash you those sweet eyes. Or she will march over and sit smack on top of the morning newspaper that you're trying to page through. This is a cat's way of saying, "Hey, look at me. Pay attention to *me. Now!*"

curious cat chat

Trick training would be much easier if people could speak "cat" or if cats could speak "people." Unfortunately, a "people to cat" or "cat to people" translation dictionary hasn't been invented yet. But don't give up. Your first feline communication clues will come from the *way* your cat speaks to you.

Some cats can be downright chatty. If you listen closely, you will detect many different tones. Each vocal sound conveys a different message. And cat verbal language is pure— unlike ours, which can be filled with slang, double meanings or sarcasm. Cats clearly say exactly what's on their minds.

Some cats—especially Siamese ones—vocalize more than others. But, in general, the following translations work for the four most common cat-chat sounds:

- **The marvelous meow.** Your cat makes this trademark sound when she wants your attention. She may be saying, "Hey, why is my bowl empty?" or, "My favorite toy mouse got batted under the couch. I need your long arms to retrieve it." Her meows are certainly aimed at getting you to do something or react to something, but they are not spoken with any aggression.

- **The trill of the chirp.** Listen, and you may hear your cat offer up a musical trill sound that always seems to end in a question mark inflection. Cats deliver this special chirp only to people they like, never to other cats. A chirp can mean, "I'm glad you're home," or, "Why, yes, I *would* like that tasty treat you're holding in your hand."

- **The pureness of the purr.** When cats feel like they are in cat heaven, they will uncontrollably let loose a full-throttle purr that sounds like a diesel truck engine or a distant, rumbling thunderstorm. But cats also purr when they are confronted with an extremely stressful situation, such as being poked and prodded by a veterinarian. Much of why and how cats purr remains a mystery, but we do know this: Cats purr with their mouths closed while inhaling and exhaling through their noses. This is a trick that people can't do. Try piercing your lips together and purr like a cat while you breathe in and out through your nose. You will find it's easier to chew gum, make hand circles on your belly and tap the top of your head while reciting the alphabet—backwards!

- **The heart of the hiss.** Plain and simple, this heavy-on-the-S sound comes when a cat warns you to "back off." Hissing is an early warning signal, used by a cat before she starts nipping or swatting. Enough said.

- **The long M–O–A–N.** This elongated "O" or "U" panic or protest call comes from a cat about to regurgitate a hairball or one resisting restrain during a veterinary exam. Clearly, this cat is not content.

body language basics

Congratulations! You now understand basic cat chat. Next comes another communication hurdle: What if your cat behaves like a furry mime, barely uttering a mini-mew? What do you do?

First, study your cat's posture and motions. Cats speak more with their bodies than with their vocal chords. And they do most of their communicating with body movements. Alas, you don't have a tail or whiskers, but you *can* gain your cat's appreciation if you learn to read and react accordingly to these primary cat body cues:

- **Hail the tail.**  You can sense your cat's mood just by noticing the position of her tail. True, tails provide balance for our agile friends, but tails also signal their moods. Certainly, we know that a cat feels spooked or startled when she puffs out her tail like a pipe cleaner.

But here are a few more "true tails": Confident and contented cats will hold their tails loosely upright when they walk. If they twitch the top of their upright tail at you, they are sending you sweet greetings. Angry cats twitch their stiff tails side to side or loudly thump their tails on the floor. Clearly, they are not happy with the current scene—such as witnessing the neighborhood cat spray the living room window with urine when they are watching from the inside and can't react or attack.

- **Aye, aye, the eyes.** Those golden, emerald or powder-blue eyes never mask a cat's feelings. Study their eyes. Nervous, agitated or downright angry cats will deliver glares and dilated pupils. It's a cat's way of warning you to back off. Happy, content purr-machines will greet you with half-opened, winking eyes. Among cats, this sweet greeting is filled with pure love.

- **Now ear this.** Cats who are receptive to you and pay attention to your training methods will tend to point their ears forward and slightly outward. This means that Kitty is tuning in to your verbal cues. But a frustrated or unwilling cat will flatten her ears tightly against her head.

- **Here's the real rub.** When a cat brushes her torso against your calf or grazes her cheekbone against your extended hand, she is marking you. This is a form of feline flattery that alerts other scent-savvy animals within range that, "Hey, this is *mine*."

the universal language

In any partnership, success relies on how well the two parties speak the same language. By understanding cat chat and feline body cues, you will strengthen your communication skills with your cat. This is very important for successful trick training.

The cornerstone of successful training is positive reinforcement. Most cats are willing students when they can work for food rewards. Cats need to know there will be a payoff for their performances.

Begin any training session by addressing your cat by name. This alerts her that you are talking to her—not to the dog, your spouse or the ballgame on television.

When your cat glides into the room and comes into view, offer a friendly greeting and call her by name. Say, "Hey, Kitty, it's good to see you." Use her name often so that she learns to associate hearing you speak her name with happy actions such as getting praise or receiving a tasty treat.

Speak in calm, soothing tones so she will feel special and a part of the family. Your cat will quickly learn how to interpret your voice tones and body cues if you are consistent as to how you deliver them.

Engage more in two-way chatting instead of one-way directives such as, "Time to take your pill, Kitty," or, "Kitty, get down from the kitchen counter—*now*." Try saying something like, "Hey, Kitty, let's practice your 'Sit' command. I've got a tasty treat in my hand just for you." Guess what? You just got your cat's attention!

In addition, try making cat sounds such as little meows or chirps. Even if your feeble meow attempts are pure nonsense, your cat will appreciate your efforts. Just avoid hissing at her.

a dozen cat-trick-training commandments

If only you could wave a wand and—poof!—your cat is a trick performer. Alas, success depends on many ministeps and plenty of practice. In fact, there are 12 informal rules that will make training easier and more enjoyable for both of you:

1. Always begin training by speaking your cat's name in an upbeat, positive tone to catch her attention and interest.

2. Enter each training session with an attitude that is positive, patient and encouraging. You will set the tone for learning.

3. Time training sessions for when your cat is most receptive to learning, and *not* when training is most convenient to your schedule. Cats waking up from naps are usually a little hungry and are more likely to want to learn (and eat treats) than cats who have just polished off an entire bowl of kibble and now want to sit in a sunny corner and groom themselves.

4. Select a quiet room where you can have uninterrupted time with your cat. Try to

remove as many distractions (the TV, the radio, the dog) as you can.

5. Be consistent with your verbal and hand-signal commands. Use the same gesture time after time for every command. Don't mix up your signals, or your cat will be very confused.

6. Immediately provide food rewards and praise for each success, no matter how small. And don't delay. Treats should be instant—within a second or two of your cat's mini-triumph. This will reinforce to your feline student the connection between the trick and the treat.

7. Teach your cat only one new trick at a time. Cats are not multitaskers. So start by teaching her the basics, such as "Come" (see chapter 1) or "Sit" (see chapter 2). Work on one command until your cat masters it. Then, on another training day, introduce a second basic trick.

8. Build on the basics. Once your cat knows simple commands, gradually introduce more advanced commands such as, "Go find your mouse under the couch," or, "Go to the back door if you want to go outside for a walk on a leash."

9. Limit each training session to 5 or 10 minutes—or even less. Cats don't have long attention spans, and with their heightened senses of smell, sight and hearing, they are apt to get distracted by things you aren't aware of.

10. Be adaptable and flexible. Acknowledge that there will be times when your cat simply isn't in the mood to learn or perform a trick.

11. Set your cat up for success, even if it's an itty-bitty accomplishment. This will build her confidence. If your cat isn't performing the desired behavior, chances are good that you are moving too quickly. Make sure that your cat understands each training step before you progress to the next one.

12. Tap into your cat's innate curiosity and instinctive drive. As born predators, cats love to chase, stalk and capture. Introduce tricks that feature these natural feline tendencies. Once your cat has mastered the basics, you are limited only by your imagination—and teaching technique— as to the more-difficult tricks that you introduce to your cat.

a meow-valous finish

Food treats definitely rate high on every cat's wish list, but don't underestimate the power of touch. Cats usually prefer therapeutic massages to ordinary tap-tap-taps on their heads or quick slaps on their backs.

Massage offers both physical and mental benefits. The right touch improves the flow of rich, oxygenated blood throughout your cat's body. It increases range of motion and flexibility. It also helps to detect any lumps, cuts, fleas or ticks so that you can remedy these situations in their early stages.

Beyond the physical benefits, massage also builds trust and friendship between you and your cat. It can even improve behavior in aloof or skittish felines.

Just follow these guidelines to ensure that your cat reaps the maximum benefits from massage sessions:

- Allow your cat to pick the time to receive a massage.

- Let your cat select a comfortable place. Top cat choices include the sofa, the foot of your bed, a wide windowsill or a plush carpet.

- Approach your cat slowly and speak to her in soothing tones. Let her know that it's massage time.

- Pay attention to your cat's body language to detect her receptiveness. Sleepy, half-eyed looks or gentle nudges are signals that your cat wants a massage. Stop massaging your cat if she gives you a full-pupil glare or a loud yowl, or if she wiggles out of your arms. These are all signs that Kitty isn't in the massage mood.

- Don't use fancy oils, creams or lotions. And make sure that your hands are clean and dry.

- Never use your fingernails. Instead, use your palms or fingertips to knead, flick, rub, glide and stroke.

- Stroke Kitty's muscles in the direction of her heart to improve blood flow.

- Rely on an airy touch, a light caress or mild strokes. Never press too deeply.

- Match the speed of your movement to the mood of your cat. A cat just waking up from an afternoon snooze may prefer gentle, relaxed strokes. A cat just finishing a frisky play session may seek faster, firmer strokes.

- Limit massage sessions to 5 to 10 minutes—or even less if your cat acts restless.

it's showtime!

Will all this trick training guarantee that your feline friend becomes the next Hollywood cat celebrity? Probably not. The true idea behind trick training is to build a stronger bond and to develop a deeper level of trust with your cat. Interactive play will stimulate your cat's mind and strengthen her self-confidence—as well as her muscles. When you prove yourself as a truly caring, patient teacher, don't be surprised if your cat seeks you out to work on a trick. Ready to learn? Read on!

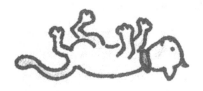

come hither

Veteran cat owners fondly share a saying
with rookie cat owners: "Dogs come
when they're called. Cats will take a message
and get back to you later." But there is no
reason that this saying should apply to *your*
cat. Being far more independent than their
canine counterparts, cats need a darn good
reason for being beckoned by you into a
room. You have to be patient, persistent and
positive. Make this one of the very first tricks
you teach your kitten or newly adopted cat.
It can literally save one or more of his nine
lives—especially if he slips out the front door.
A cat who comes when called can skirt the

dangers of the outside world—such as the neighbor's dog or speedy motorists. Having your cat come when you call him is definitely an action you want to become a habit.

rendezvous in the kitchen

The best time to teach the "Come" command is at mealtime in the kitchen. After all, a kitchen to a cat is a *meow*-valous place full of tasty delights. In fact, without even realizing it, you may already be conditioning your cat to come on cue. Before you set his bowl down, chances are good that he is already sitting pretty or snaking his body around your legs in eager anticipation.

Each time you open a cat-food can with an electric can opener or by pulling the metal tab back, your cat learns to associate these sounds with food. Use this magical bond between cats and can-opening sounds to your advantage.

the trifecta: tap, whistle & call

There are three tools to assist you in getting your cat to come when summoned. For starters, let's use the arsenal in the kitchen.

Before you open a new can of cat food or begin to pour some dry food into Tiger's bowl, either tap the empty bowl with a metal spoon a few times or give a small canister of treats a few shakes as Tiger approaches the kitchen. Call your cat by name: "Tiger, come." When your cat arrives, dote on him and give him lots of praise. Then make a big production out of pouring the kibble or spooning the canned food into his bowl. Feed him and gently pet him for a few seconds.

Outside the kitchen and between meals, reinforce the "Come" command by stocking your front pocket with a few of your cat's favorite treats. Do not give treats at any other time except when you are training your cat.

Always say your cat's name before saying, "Come." What you are doing is first getting your cat's attention and then letting him know that good things happen when you say his name. In the beginning, even if he only takes a few steps toward you and stops, praise and treat him so he sees the connection. Hand over treats each time your cat comes until he is consistent. Later on, you can treat him to calorie-free praise and cuddling.

Some cats ignore your voice, so here's a backup plan: Whistle. Make it a distinctive upbeat tune, perhaps the opening notes of "Jingle Bells." It's okay to feel a little silly while you whistle this way. But having a unique whistle is vital, especially if your cat dashes out of your house. Some indoor cats become quite frightened by the big, bad outside world. Your private whistle lets them know that it is you, their trusted friend, who is calling for them to come back. And cats in training want to again remind you to provide them with treats when they respond to your whistling.

take a seat

t he "Sit" trick ranks high on the list of training commands. It is a basic building block to a score of many other cool tricks. Once a cat can sit on cue, she becomes much more receptive to learning other tricks and good behaviors. A cat that sits displays good manners and conveys respect toward you, her benevolent tutor.

under the sit spell

Let me share with you a secret long held by dog trainers. The easiest way to teach a dog— or a cat, or even a bunny rabbit—to "Sit" on command is to let gravity be your ally. You

don't need to be a whiz at physics to make gravity work to your advantage.

First, choose a quiet place in your home, a place where your cat feels comfy and cozy and, most of all, safe. What you are doing is establishing an atmosphere conducive to fun learning.

Give your cat a few cuddles and head scratches to make her feel at ease. Hoist her up on a table so you can work this trick without having to bend *way* down. Some cats can be intimidated by a person who looms over them, casting a shadow—even if it's their owner.

Speak to your cat in a friendly, chatty tone while she gets used to being on the table. Then place a small food treat between your thumb and index finger. Hold the treat right in front of your cat's nose. Let her get a good whiff. (Watch out—some cats may begin to drool in anticipation!)

Now, this is the part of the trick where gravity enters the scene. With your cat in a standing position, slowly bring the treat up and over your cat's head while saying her name and giving the command, "Sit." Your food-motivated cat will automatically tip her head back to follow the path of the treat. In order to maintain her

balance, she will have to sit down. That's the beauty behind the law of physics.

Once your cat plants her rump on the table top, say, "Sit, good, sit," and immediately give her the food treat.

Repeat these steps until your cat obeys the "Sit" command without you holding a treat over her head. All she needs as a cue will be your hand moving slowly over her head.

Troubles on the tabletop? Not a problem. If your cat does not sit when you ask her to, gently press down on her back end as you say her name and, "Sit." Be gentle and patient so you do not frighten or frustrate your cat.

on the top of the world

When your cat has become a "Sit" expert, she will easily assume the position on the tabletop and the kitchen floor. That's your signal that she is ready for graduate school of "Sit". This advanced version of the basic "Sit" command taps into your cat's innate desire and ability to leap and land.

Select a bar stool or kitchen chair as your training tool. At mealtime, place your cat's food bowl on the chair. Get her into the routine of eating from this perch. She is learning that only positive things, like getting fed, occur in this chair. This chair is viewed as a place of goodness and security.

Between meals, remove the food bowl from the chair. Shake a treat canister to get your cat's attention.

As she enters the room, remove a treat from the canister and move slowly toward the chair to make sure that she is capturing the entire sequence. Hold the treat about one foot directly above the chair. Say her name and, "Up" and tap the seat with your other hand. Once your cat leaps up on the chair, immediately say her name and, "Sit." Once she sits, give her the treat. Repeat this a few times each training session.

Eventually, your super-smart cat will learn to leap on the chair with you only tapping the seat in silence and to promptly get into a "Sit" position the second you begin to guide the treat over her head.

a shoulder to jump on

many cats are natural born leapers and can already jump very high at an early age. These felines are the ones to whom you can most easily teach the "Shoulder" trick. This trick involves getting your cat to jump up onto your shoulder from the floor, on your either verbal or gestured command.

is your cat a shoulder cat?

Before you begin teaching your cat to jump on your shoulder, you may want to let him ride around on it to see whether or not he is a "shoulder" cat. While many cats prefer to be slung over your shoulder when you hold them (similar to the position of burping a baby), other cats do not like to be held this way and will claw at you. Instead, these cats may prefer to be cradled in your arms—or not be held at all. If this is the case for your cat, you will first need to get him comfortable with either being held or being perched on your shoulder.

As with any cat, the younger he is when you start the teaching process, the quicker he will catch on.

one leap at a time

To teach Mittens to jump on your shoulder, start out slowly by sitting on the floor. Make sure that both you and your cat are in a comfortable position. Next, pat your shoulder (whichever shoulder you want him to jump on). At the same time, you can use a verbal command, such as "Shoulder!" Be sure to use a positive, encouraging tone.

Once you have gotten your cat to jump the short distance from the floor to your shoulder (while you are sitting on the floor), praise him  and give him a favorite feline treat. Be certain that your cat understands exactly why he is being rewarded!

onward & upward

Next, take the shoulder jump to a slightly higher position: Sit on a chair while your cat remains on the floor. If your cat doesn't jump up on your shoulder this time, you can lean over and try the command again. Once Mittens has managed that distance, sit upright in the chair and coax him to jump onto your shoulder yet again. Eventually— with a lot of praise and many special treats— you and your cat will have completed the second step of the trick-teaching process.

At long last, stand in an upright position with your cat sitting in front of you—looking up at you and hopefully waiting for the command that you have so patiently taught him. Pat your shoulder and give your verbal command (if you have chosen to use one). If your kitty is ready for this final step, he will leap onto your shoulder without a moment's hesitation. Your friends and family will be amazed at how smart and how much fun your Mittens is!

if mittens misses

Of course, don't be too disappointed if Mittens "misses" the first few times. Even though cats are excellent judges of distance, it may take several tries before he gets the hang of this trick. Trust is crucial—for both you and your cat—in teaching this trick. Mittens must trust that, if he doesn't quite reach your shoulder, he will not fall because your loving arms will catch him. And you must trust your cat to not maul you with his claws if he accidentally misses the intended target.

ding-dong!

"Knock, knock."

"Who's there?"

"Um . . . it's me, your cat. Could you please open the door?"

If only life were that simple. Unfortunately, cats can't tell us in words what they want. However, they often *can* communicate their needs to us in other ways. If we are able to teach our feline companions *how* to tell us— in ways that we understand—what they want and need, all doors, including those of communication, are sure to open!

speaking of doors . . .

Inside your house, there are doors that you keep shut for many reasons, but will gladly open for your cat if she wants to see what's on the other side. Of course, your cat probably knows *exactly* what's on the other side of that door—and every other one in your house. But as a cat, she believes that it's her right to find out *at this very moment*. So if you teach Kitty a trick that allows her to tell you exactly what she wants, you can cut to

the chase *and,* at the same time, instill in her some polite behavior. Therefore, if your cat wants to see what's on the other side of that door *at this exact moment,* she should have the good manners to "knock" first.

One very important point I need to make is that this trick is *not* intended for doors to the *outside!* Indoor cats are healthier and happier, and have a much longer life span than cats who are allowed outside. So please don't even consider letting your cat outside unless, of course, you have her on a leash. (See chapter 6 for how to leash-train your kitty.) Keeping in mind that I do not believe in the outdoor cat, a couple of commonly closed inside doors where you may let Kitty ring for entry are the basement, a screened-in porch, a seasonal sunroom, or an attic. Virtually any door that will not be open all the time will do. Make sure that your basement and attic are cat-proofed and equipped with food, water and a litter box.

ignoring the plaintive meow

By the way, a cat who meows when she wants something may seem cute at first, but please do not encourage this behavior. Your cat will quickly figure out that her pitiful

cries work for *everything*. And then you are sure to run crazily around your house, trying to figure out exactly what each plaintive meow means. For the ornery cat—and there are a few out there—this meow may just be part of a larger game to see if her person (you) will get up off the couch and follow her around. Trust me, it's much better to teach your cat distinct tricks for each of her needs.

let me in!

The easiest way your cat can tell you when she wants to go into in a room behind a closed door is for you to hang a bell on the doorknob. Almost every cat—no matter what her IQ—will understand this trick without much fuss.

All you have to do is hang a bell (almost any type of bell that rings when your cat bats it will do) on the doorknobs of all rooms that you *will* let your cat into when she rings the bell. As an added enticement, lure your cat to the door using one of her favorite treats. Then, when Kitty bats the bell—it's snack time! Treats are sure to pique her interest in both door and bell—and in you!

Remember that consistency is the key to teaching your cat every trick in this book! If you are inconsistent and only let your cat into a room *some* of the time, she won't associate ringing the bell with getting into the room.

Also, if there's a room that you don't always want your cat to go into (for example, the porch, which gets too cold during the winter), take the bell *off* the doorknob until the cat *can* go in (like when the weather outside warms up a bit).

However, it's not a good idea to practice this "on/off" scenario on a regular basis. The only way your cat will comprehend *why* she is performing these tricks is if you are consistent. And when there is no reward—if your cat doesn't get into the room when she rings the doorbell—she is sure to lose interest in both door and bell.

Once your cats masters this trick, guests will be amazed when your cat rings the bell for entry into a particular room—perhaps to enjoy some bird-watching? And what could be better than impressing your guests? Aside from pleasing your cat, that is.

the ladder climb

most cats are natural-born climbers. So it's no surprise that teaching your cat how to climb up a ladder is pretty simple—not to mention quick!

humble beginnings

Start out small when you teach your cat how to climb a ladder—no matter how much of an acrobat he already is. I recommend using anything with only a few levels to climb— perhaps a stepladder or a kitchen stool.

Note: Always use a wooden ladder for this trick—if your cat slips for some reason, he can use his claws to catch himself on a wooden ladder, but not on an aluminum or fiberglass one.

The best way to entice your cat up a ladder is with a feather toy that you can control on the end of a stick. As your cat reaches out for the toy on the first step, move the toy up to the next step, then the next, and so on. If you use a small stepladder during the first few attempts at this trick, your cat should soon find himself on the top of the world. Reward him generously when he reaches the summit of his stepladder. Either give him a treat, or lavish him with praise and petting. Of course, you must also let him finally catch the "prey" that he spent so much time chasing . . .

After your cat has conquered a small ladder, increase the size of the ladder until you find one the perfect one for your cat to climb. Use a ladder that folds out and has actual slats, rather than a rung-type ladder (also known as an extension ladder) where the cat must advance up a series of rod-shaped—and sometimes very slippery—steps. Climbing down this type of ladder can be virtually impossible—as well as dangerous—for cats lacking top-notch coordination skills. It's better to be safe now than sorry later.

Keep in mind: This is *not* a safe trick to teach a declawed cat. A cat who has been declawed may be able to climb *up* certain objects—but he probably won't get a good hold on his way back *down.* In general, teaching tricks to a declawed cat may take some extra research and patience. After all, claws are very important to a cat's balance—both physical and mental.

getting down

Okay, so your beloved fur-face is looking down at you from the top level of—for example—a six-foot, fold-out stepladder . . . now what?

Well, climbing up the ladder was the easy part. Getting your cat back down may be a more difficult task. But it's not impossible! First of all, most cats like the being above it all (so to speak). Cats feel safe high up off the ground where they can scan the surrounding area for danger—and keep an eye out for that monstrous, noisy machine you drag across the carpet every now and then. So your feline may want to lounge at the top of the ladder for a while. And you should let him.

When you and your cat finally agree that it's time to descend, you can use the same toy on a stick to get him to back down again. Remember, it is probably going to be scarier for him to come down that ladder (just as it is for many people) because he has to look where he's going. And depending on the size of the ladder, it may appear to be a very long way down.

exercise love & patience

Don't pressure your cat into coming down too quickly—or you could turn him off ladder-climbing for good. If the toy method doesn't work for your cat on the way back down, place a tasty treat on each step to entice him more convincingly. When your cat finally masters the delicate art of climbing and descending ladders of various sizes, you can proudly show off his amazing ability—and

agility—to all your friends and family. Some people may want to leave the ladder out—making sure it's securely grounded to prevent it from tipping over—because it makes an inexpensive playground for the acrobat cat. However, getting your kitty to perform this trick on demand might be more difficult if he has around-the-clock access to his very own private jungle gym.

Regardless, once you watch your cat scratch and claw his way to the top of that long ladder of success, it will all be worth it. Just look at him, perched proudly on his pedestal!

on the cat walk

When most people imagine strolling through the park with a furry friend by their side, that furry friend is a dog. And why wouldn't he be? Who ever heard of walking a cat on a leash? Cats won't walk on a leash. They're cats, right?

Hogwash! Cats *can* be trained to walk on a leash. And it's not that hard to teach them. In fact, someday it might be very common to see felines and their people strolling side-by-side alfresco.

As with any trick you teach your cat, the younger your cat, the easier it will be to teach her. However, the myth that you can't teach an old dog—or, in this case, an old cat—new tricks is simply that . . . a myth! No matter how old your cat, walking her on a leash can be an enjoyable experience for both of you—as long as Fluffy is correctly leash-trained.

the great indoors

It is absolutely imperative that all training sessions take place indoors in a room where your cat feels safe and secure. If you try to take Fluffy outside to show her the rewards she will reap by walking on a leash, she will either be enticed beyond belief by the many new sights and sounds, or she will be irreparably spooked. Your cat may become so mesmerized by her new (outdoor) surround-ings, that your commands will be nothing more than background noise.

Of course, Fluffy has seen all those infe-rior creatures (also known as dogs) walk-ing around the neighborhood on a length of rope. So the first thought to enter her mind may be, "You've got to be kidding!" And unlike a dog, your kitty probably won't come running eagerly (at least not at first) when she hears her leash taken out of the closet.

harnessing talent

Walking a cat on a leash that's attached to her collar can be dangerous. A regular collar can easily choke a cat, and a cat can easily wriggle out of a regular collar. Attaching a leash to a harness that fits around her body is more secure.

The harness method is a two-dimensional training technique. First, you need to get your kitty comfortable with the harness. Like a collar, a harness needs to fit snugly, but not *too* snugly—you should be able to comfortably stick a finger between the harness and the cat's body.

Now comes the next—and slightly more difficult—part. You must convince your cat that walking on a leash is great fun. And how do you do this? Patience and timing are key:

1. First, put the harness on your cat for short periods of time, then reward her with praise or treats for her good behavior.

2. After she is comfortable wearing the harness, you can attach the leash to it.

Remember: It's best to do this for short periods of time and reward your kitty for remaining calm.

Once you and your cat *both* feel comfortable leash walking around the house, it's time to take the plunge and go outside. At first, Fluffy may be intimidated by the vastness of the great outdoors. Be patient and let her explore all those new sights and smells.

Never drag your cat on her leash. If you drag her, she will have a negative reaction to leash walking. And then all the energy you spent teaching her this trick will be for naught.

Remember to give your cat time to adapt to leash walking. Your cat will become the perfect leash-walking companion *only when she is ready*. And not a moment sooner! As with *any* trick, if your cat does not want to walk on a leash after calm, repeated attempts, do not *force* her to perform something she is

dead-set against. Doing so will only damage—and perhaps even destroy—the trusting relationship between you and your feline friend.

Teaching your cat to walk on a leash can be a way for both of you to spend more quality time together. And not only will you be getting exercise and fresh air, but you'll also show the world that leashes aren't just for dogs anymore.

pucker up

When you were a child, your parents probably warned you about kissing your kitty. They may have said, "Do you know where his mouth has been?" This obviously was a reference to feline self-grooming— a perfectly natural part of Kitty's frequent bathing routine. As children, it wasn't a big deal—most of us just kissed our kitty when no one was looking.

kissing kitty

But as cat-loving adults, we *do* know where our cat's mouths have been. And, yes—even if

it's a little gross—a smooch from Kitty is still one of the greatest gifts that he can give you.

There are several types of kitty kisses that you can receive. Some people still object to an on-the-lips kiss. If that's your case, you can always teach kitty to kiss your nose or cheek.

It may be true that cats don't express their affection as openly as dogs do. But this doesn't mean that felines don't feel love toward their people. Instead, they just may need a bit more prompting—and prodding—before they kiss the hand that feeds them. Don't despair! Follow these five easy steps for smooching success:

1. Sit at the same level as your kitty. Being face to face with him (on the floor) is best.

2. Associate a sound or a signal to tell your cat when it's time for the "kissing routine." The best signal is the universal kissing sound. (You know this sound—it's the sound you make when you pucker up and smooch the air!)

3. Now make the kissing sound. Slowly move toward your cat, all the while continuing to make the kissing sound.

4. Hold a treat next to where you want Kitty to smooch. Your feline is sure to follow. Another very enticing way to grab your cat's attention is to take a sip of milk. The smell is sure to attract him!

5. Once your cat kisses you on the nose or cheek (or forehead or chin), immediately give him a treat—along with praise and petting—for a job well done.

up close & personal

Although this trick is rather simple in concept, it won't work with all cats. Some shy or reserved cats may have a problem getting up close and personal with their people.

If your cat resists all your attempts to smooch, do *not* force him! We all know how yucky an unwanted kiss can be. And since you will be face to face with your cat, he might reject you with a scratch—or even a bite! You don't want him to feel threatened—and a person's face can sometimes be a scary thing. Always be careful and considerate when you kiss your cat.

with love & kisses

Knowing your kitty's unique personality will help you decide if you want to—and if you *can*—teach him this trick. If you do manage to teach your cat to smooch, you are a lucky person indeed. Just picture it—you walk into your home, make the kissing sound, and then watch as Kitty runs up to you full of love—and kisses.

it's dinnertime!

mealtime in a pet owner's home can be a happy occasion as family members gather around the table to eat and talk about their day. It can also be a time of forceful reprimands directed toward the family pet over who gets to eat the food intended for people.

The second scenario—a cat (or a dog) begging and whining for people food—is an unpleasant experience. But you *can* train your pet (cats are easier to train since they are finicky eaters) to eat when it's *her* dinnertime, not yours. The trick is to teach Whiskers which signs indicate her meal is being served!

the din of dinner

Some people think it's cute to clink a spoon against the side of Whiskers's bowl to let her know when dinner is  served. And when Whiskers comes running at this (not-so-unusual) sound, it might seem as though you've taught your cat a trick: how to come for her supper.

Except that there's a little problem here . . . Whiskers will soon come running whenever you clink a glass in your kitchen. So if you eat a bowl of ice cream, or stir some crackers into your cup of soup, Whiskers will think it's time to eat.

If you don't want to wear out poor Whiskers—not to mention yourself—you have to do two things. First, you have to keep Whiskers out of the kitchen or dining room while you eat. And second, you need to create a *special* signal or sound for Whiskers's mealtime. Don't use this sound for anything else, or Whiskers will be confused and the signal will lose its meaning.

The best way to call your cat for dinner is by ringing a bell. You will need to find an

unusual sounding bell—one that isn't heard every day and one that you won't use for anything *except* for Whiskers's dinner call. If you accidentally ring Whiskers's bell and she comes running, you should feed her a little token treat (even if it isn't her mealtime). As any cat owner will tell you, consistency is everything!

food wars

You can easily avoid fighting with Whiskers over people food if you stick to your guns:

- Never feed Whiskers table scraps. *Remember:* Cats are extremely finicky. If they are accustomed to eating greasy hamburgers or broiled lobster, they may never be satisfied with "boring" cat food again. This isn't fair to (or healthy for) your favorite feline.

- Keep her bowl(s) out of the kitchen.

- Put Whiskers in her own special room during mealtime.

- Feed her while you and your family eat— but *not* in the same room.

Use the special signal that tells Whiskers without a doubt when her—and only her— dinner is served. Be patient and persistent. And, of course, provide Whiskers with her favorite cat-food brand and flavor.

shake on it

the "Shake" command is most often associated with the canine species, but this is not a difficult trick to teach your cat. Because felines are much more apt to use their paws to pick up or move things, they will learn this trick perhaps even more quickly than Rover. A dog will usually use her nose to push an object or her mouth to pick it up, but cats are naturally paw-oriented.

Showing off how your cat can "Shake" on command will probably surprise and astonish your friends and family because this is normally a trick performed exclusively by your kitty's canine counterpart. But, since your cat already knows he is superior to the dog class, Boots should be eager to introduce himself to the guests who visit your home—particularly those who are self-proclaimed canine aficionados. Witnessing that cats are able to learn the same basic commands as dogs should win over all those skeptics who believe cats cannot learn tricks—or at least can't learn them as effectively as dogs.

which paw?

Experts have researched the topic of left-pawed versus right-pawed felines for quite some time. While many believe that the majority of cats are left-pawed (meaning that they favor their left paw to touch or pick up objects), only *you* can be the final authority on your furry friend's favored paw. It may be that Boots is ambidextrous and does not favor either front paw but instead uses them both equally.

pleased to meet you

To start out, make sure that your cat is in a sitting position, then simply touch one of his paws and say, "Shake." Once his paw is touched, your cat will probably lift it up of

the floor. Once it's in the air, gently take it in your hand and shake it. Then give him a food reward and praise him when he performs the "Shake" command. After a few rounds, your cat *should* have this trick mastered—paws down!

One important point to make is that you don't want Boots to think you are playing a game with him. Otherwise, the paw that comes up to shake your delicate hand may have claws extended and ready to scratch instead of shake.

Repeat the steps for the "Shake" command exactly as you originally began the teaching phase and your cat will most likely learn this simple trick without too much difficulty.

An open mind, as well as plenty of love and patience, should soon have Boots ready to "Shake" whenever you—or your guests— greet him upon entering your abode. If any- thing can truly make a house into a *home*, it is most definitely being greeted each and every day with a paw-shake from your loyal feline companion. This end result can—and will—happen as long as you follow the above techniques. And, of course, never force your cat to train when he doesn't want to.

roll over like rover

When it comes to performing 360-degree belly rolls on the kitchen floor for treats, dogs dominate. But step aside, Fido. This feat can also be easily mastered by any food-motivated feline.

The best cat candidates are those that easily flop on the floor in front of your stride and sweetly gaze up at you with those "feed-me-pet-me-please" eyes. Even better— the cat that automatically meets you half-way: one that flops on the floor and goes belly up for a desired tummy rub. It is as if your cat is sending you cues that it is trick-and-treat time.

a successful flop

For this trick, timing is oh-so vital. Improve your chances for success by introducing this trick when your cat is just—*yawn*—stretching from one of her numerous afternoon catnaps or is impatiently ushering you into the kitchen for a feed-me-*now* tasty treat.

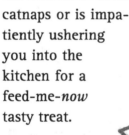

A sleepy cat is willing to let gravity guide her to the ground, and a hungry cat is willing to give you her total attention in hopes of chewing on some delightful dividends.

Break down this trick into little steps and build on each minor success. Heap on the praise and the treats along the way until you can have your cat drop, flop and roll in one fluid motion—preferably in front of house-guests you wish to wow. (I love hearing the phrase, "Are you sure you don't have a dog dressed in cat's clothing?").

Some cats are all ears; for others, their eyes rule their universe. Rely on both hand signals and verbal cues. Each reinforces the other. And be consistent: Use the same hand motion and the same words each and every time. Once your cat knows this trick in her sleep, you can then try having her perform by using only one cue.

drop, flop & roll

Kneel in front of your cat as she sits on the floor. Give her a sweet cat wink and speak in an upbeat tone. You've captured her attention.

Hold a small treat in your right hand. Give her a few seconds to eye the treat to spark her interest. Slowly guide the little nibble of food counterclockwise over your cat's left shoulder to the point that she must swivel her head to continue to look at it.

Say, "Roll over," as you keep moving your hand up and over her shoulder and toward the floor. When your cat tries to snag the treat with her paws, the laws of physics kick in. Her belly will automatically go up, and she will roll over on her side. If your cat looks a little spooked, gently cajole her by nudging her top front leg to the other side and saying "Roll over."

Don't delay—hand over the treat. Allow her plenty of time to chew and swallow before continuing. Remember, you need to reward each small victory!

With your cat flopped on her side, use a new treat positioned under her nose and continue moving slowly counterclockwise until she is back into a "Sit" or "four-on-the-floor" position. Again, reward with a treat.

Practice this trick daily but limit each class session to five minutes or less. Cats crave routine, but *please,* don't go overboard, or you will risk boring your cat. She may simply stand up and strut out of the room with her tail pointed up in the air. Class is over.

roll over review

Your cat may flawlessly perform the "Roll Over" trick a dozen times in a week without a miss. Then, suddenly, she will stop in mid-flop and give you a big look of confusion. She may have been distracted by the loud

barking of your neighbor's dog, by the whiff of the tuna casserole bubbling in your oven or by the sight of a very clumsy but friendly child headed her way. Or the cause for the ruined "Roll Over" may never be known.

Don't panic. Just start back at the beginning. Build on each mini-victory until your cat's memory kicks in and she is back to flip-flopping her way to fun.

kitty keep-away

i f cats required résumés, leaping and grab-
bing would top the list of their skills. And
don't forget the innate need to show off such
prowess. This trick provides the *purr*-fect venue
for jock cats. Like dogs who aim to drool and
please, cats like to display their agile abilities
in front of an awed audience. For this trick,
the audience need only be you and another
person. And the best part: All you need is a
small cat toy that you can send airborne.

flying mouse overhead!

Fun-seeking cats don't always want to be
solo acts. This trick requires interaction

with people in order for your cat to truly engage. Your cat gets to grab the spotlight; you get the chance to strengthen your friendship bond with your cat (which may move you up a few notches in the "cool person" barometer).

Take an inventory of your cat's toys. Your quest: to find one of your cat's favorite toys. Odds are that your cat's all-time admired toy is always tucked under the stove, buried under the newspaper on the living room floor or stashed under your bed pillow for safekeeping. So be diligent in your search.

Why is it so important to determine your cat's favorite toy? Motivation. For this trick, you want the gotta-have-it toy that your cat totally craves. The toy must also be small and lightweight. (You don't want to throw out your shoulder.) The toy should be easy for you to toss and easy for your airborne cat to snag midflight.

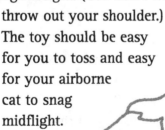

toy–tossing 101

Select an open area in your house. You need clear floor space without any objects (such as a potted plant or a sofa) in the way. Bring a handful of your cat's favorite food treat divided into itty-bitty pieces to offer as mini-rewards.

Sit on the floor and have a cat-friendly friend or family member sit directly across from you about 6 to 10 feet away. The floor between you should be wide open. Call your cat by his name and tempt him into the room by displaying his favorite toy or paper wad in your had. Say, "Look." If necessary, crumple the paper wad between your fingers to capture his total attention.

Coax your cat into the midpoint between you and the other person by placing a food treat on the floor. When your cat begins to eat the treat, that's the signal for the game to begin.

Lightly toss the toy or paper wad so that it sails over your cat's head and travels the distance to reach your friend. Toss at a height that clears your cat's head by a few inches—just enough to trigger his interest. Be patient. You may need to toss the toy back and forth a few times before your cat catches on. Each time, if he even looks like he is about to lunge at the airborne object, give him praise and a small treat.

Once your cat begins to leap and paw at the toy, the game is kicked into high gear. Congratulate your cat each time he "scores."

Got a super four-footed athlete up for a true challenge? Vary the height and speed of your tosses so that your cat must use his split-second reactive skills to capture this "prey."

Keep tossing the toy back and forth until your cat signals the game has ended. You'll know this because he will either start grooming himself or simply leave the room. That's a cat's way of telling you, "Hey, it's been fun, folks, but it's time for me to look glamorous—or grab a nap." Don't be offended. Your cat is just on to other activities.

stay a spell

We certainly live in a mobile society, and cats are no exception. They aren't dashing off to work or to the mall, but they certainly cover lots of ground (and countertops) inside our homes. But there are times when it's necessary for our cats to act like statues, when we need them to stay in place without dashing from the room. This trick is designed to benefit you during those times when you need to give your cat a pill, put on her collar, or slip her into the pet carrier for a veterinary appointment.

outfoxing a fleet-footed feline

Unless you can run like an Olympic sprinter, make hairpin turns like a ball in a pinball machine and dash under the bed without bumping your head, you will never win the game of chase with your much-more-agile cat. The solution is to outsmart your cat by teaching her the "Stay" command. To do this successfully, you need two things:

1. **Location, location, location.** Select an enclosed area such as the bathroom, den or screened porch to teach this trick. The room must be a place where your cat cannot find out-of-reach hiding spots or make like Houdini and—poof!—disappear from sight. The room must also eliminate the distractions of the wide-open living room with the TV blaring and family members moving in and out. You need to be alone with your curious cat.

2. **The right attitude.** Cats may not understand our words, but they definitely can interpret our tones and our moods. You need to be calm and confident to teach the "Stay" command to your cat. If your voice sounds impatient or hurried, your cat is less apt to be a willing student. Before you enter the room, try taking a few deep breaths, slowly inhaling and exhaling.

don't make any fast moves

Sit or kneel on the floor in the room. Be quiet for a minute or so, and let your intrigued cat approach you. Speak slowly and softly, and avoid any sudden, jerky hand motions. You want to calm your cat.

If your cat begins to move away from you, say her name followed by "Stay." Speak with authority, but do not yell.

Extend your right arm straight out. With your palm facing down, move it down steadily and slowly toward the floor as you repeat the "Stay" command.

If your cat moves away, do not chase her. Maintain your stationary position. When she returns and sits or lies down near you, gently pet her and say, "Good girl, Fluffy." Give her a friendly hug and place her back down on the floor.

You may need to offer your cat food "bribes" to convince her to stay in place. Put the treat in your hand and move it to the ground to help guide your cat into a sitting or lying down position. As she eats the treat, gently place your hand on her shoulders; say, "Good, stay," and keep her in position for five seconds before removing your hand.

Repeat these steps four or five times during each training session. When you open the door, let your cat scoot out if she wants, but you stay put for a minute or so. When you leave the room, do so slowly and leave your cat alone for about 10 minutes. This shows her that you don't plan to stalk or chase her, and that this "Stay" trick comes with praise and food payoffs.

Once your cat masters the "Stay" command in an enclosed room, begin practicing this trick in an open area. Heap on the food treats and praise each time she stays in place. The next time you have to tend to your cat, you'll be happy knowing that your chasing days are over.

hide & seek

ever get annoyed by your cat's midnight mayhem? His racing up and down your hallway or scampering up and down your stairs? Teaching this trick to your cat will unleash his kitten-like friskiness *before* you head to bed. Your cat gets the satisfaction of one-on-one playtime with you, and you stand a better chance of an uninterrupted night's sleep. Perfect!

i'll hide, you find me

The goal of this trick is to reinforce your cat's willingness to come to you on command. There is also another goal: to bolster that bond between the two of you. Playing together is a terrific way to accomplish this.

Play this game when your cat is in a playful, rambunctious, gotta-move mood—like right when you come home from work. (After all, he's been cooped up all day and is rarin' to go full throttle in front of an eager audience—you.) Be animated. (It's okay to jump up and down.) Don't worry if you look or sound a bit silly. Your exaggerated body gestures and happy tone will serve to keep your cat interested in this game. (He *promises* not to tell anyone how amusing you can be.)

Start this game in the same room as your cat. Toss a food treat across the room and away from you, making sure that your cat sees and goes after it. While he munches on the treat, quietly and quickly leave the room by slipping around the corner and out of sight. Peek around the corner and call your cat by name with enthusiasm, then dart back out of sight.

curiosity...(well, you know the rest)

Cats are curious. Your actions will definitely draw his interest. Until your cat masters this game, however, you will need an ally. Shake a canister of food treats as you say, "Tiger, nighty-night." This irresistible sound tells your cat that treats are on the way. Choosing between staying in the room or going after treats is a no-brainer for most cats.

Each time your cat races toward you, praise him and reward him with a treat. Give him some well-deserved cuddling or petting. Dash out of the room and duck around the corner a few times until your cat learns the rules of the game. Once your cat is a pro at finding you around the corner, you can increase the difficulty of your hiding places. Let him wander away, then dash behind the bathroom door or duck behind the sofa. Or race up the stairs and hide in a darkened bedroom. Each time, shake the food canister and call him by name, "Tiger, come."

three's a crowd—pleaser

Don't limit this game to just you and your cat. Once your cat knows and enjoys this game, enlist others to play this feline version of hide-and-seek.

Put your cat in one room, perhaps the kitchen or the living room. Give him a treat to eat. While he is devouring the treat, arrange for two or more people, each with a canister of treats, to sneak off into different rooms.

 Establish an order of who will call for the cat in advance. Have Caller No. 1 shake the treat can and call your cat by name. After he is rewarded with food and praise, have Caller No. 2— hiding in a different room—call for your cat.

This game hones your cat's hearing skills and re-  inforces his ability to obey the commands of others. You're training him to be obedient, but he sees this as a game. You both win.

feline floor hockey

"feline Floor Hockey" is a game that you *play with* your cat instead of a trick that you *teach to* your cat. In order to do play "Feline Floor Hockey" correctly, you need a door that closes and a room with a wood, tile or linoleum floor. (A kitchen or bathroom works best, but a small study is also fine.) The bottom of the closed door shouldn't be flush against the floor—you will need some room to push the puck around.

getting puckish

Make sure that your cat is inside a familiar, comfortable room. Shut the door and stand just outside the room. Now call your cat's name. Shake some treats in a plastic treat cup. Maybe even push one treat underneath the door to fully get your cat's attention. Once you have her attention, get out your puck.

Note: Your "puck" can be made of anything—just use your imagination. You want something that moves easily but doesn't ping crazily across the floor's surface. And you don't want anything your cat will be tempted to swallow. A rounded piece of plastic, a large marble or even a water-bottle cap all work well.

Now, slowly push the puck underneath
the closed door and wait until your cat
makes a move for it—you'll be able to tell
that she's dashing for the puck by the sound
of four paws scampering. If your cat is the
playful sort, she'll send the puck right back
underneath the door to you. So back and
forth you go.

But you don't want to bore Whiskers, do
you? So be sure to change the timing that
you return the puck to your cat. You don't
want to tease Whiskers, though—cats do not
take well to being teased! But nothing is
cuter than watching as your cat's paw
reaches up underneath the door, demanding,
"Hey! Give me my puck!"

forget me not

Some cats will completely forget about their person and begin to play hockey all by themselves. This is okay, of course. But it isn't as much fun as when you play together. So if Whiskers ignores you, just open that door and come into the room. Get control of the puck and slowly sit down on the floor. Make sure that you have your cat's full attention—if she doesn't want to share at first, toss her a treat and then show her the puck. Sit with your legs in front of you and slide the puck from side to side, making Whiskers dash to and fro, batting at it with her right paw—or her south paw—as she chooses.

food hockey

If plastic holds no appeal for your particular kitty, you might want to try playing with her food. This trick works best if you are in the same room as your cat from the very start. Of course, it goes without saying that while you're playing with your cat's food, the odds are good that once your cat gets hold of it, she will eat it. That's okay—you are just letting Whiskers know that participating in inter-species sports can be very rewarding, indeed!

Kneel in front of your cat while she sits on the floor, curiously looking at the food in your hand. Say her name, then toss the treat across the floor. The first few times you do this, your cat may just watch as the treat

slides across the room and skids underneath the refrigerator. But don't let Whiskers's inattention get you down. She's just never seen her sacred treats treated so callously! Don't worry—the confusion won't last.

Now hold a treat in your hand and allow your cat to come over and sniff it. You can even let her eat the treat. Once you have her attention, do the same with another treat. Except this time, close your hand and say, "Go get it!" as you toss the treat across the floor. Odds are, your feline will scamper after her food, paws desperately reaching for the beloved morsel. As she's about to eat her food, call your cat's name again, then toss her another treat. Toss this treat close to your cat, but don't throw it directly *at* her. Remember that this is a game; you want your cat to play this game *with* you. If you make the game too easy for Whiskers, she'll get either bored or full by the time her third treat skids across the floor.

score!

Before you know it, you may be in the kitchen—or bathroom, or study—and suddenly see a furry paw impatiently reaching underneath the door. This is a sure sign that it's feline hockey season.

not a far fetch

if you think that Rover is the only pet who can learn how to "Fetch," you obviously haven't tried teaching Socks this easy-to-learn trick. Of course, not every cat can (or will) learn every trick that you offer to teach him. So, as usual, if repeated attempts ultimately lead nowhere and you're at wit's end, maybe *then*—and only then—will your furry friend decide to teach *you* how to throw a toy so that he can bring it back and let you throw it to him again.

First of all, you need to use a favorite toy or at least something of *keen* interest to your cat. Otherwise, just like most things, Socks will simply ignore it. One of the key ingredients in getting your cat to fetch is to use something that he wants badly enough to take time out from his busy napping-and-grooming schedule to retrieve. Keep in mind that the object must be small enough to easily fit in your cat's mouth so he can carry it, but not so small that he could accidentally swallow it.

toying around . . .

With some cats, this trick may work better with a toy that they don't have 24/7 access to—something they can only play "Fetch" with. However, the downside to this is that if it's something your cat is very interested in, he may not want to share it with you—and then this trick won't work for the obvious reason: Socks will want to take said toy and spend quality time *alone* with it. The secret

to teaching Socks to successfully retrieve is to know his unique personality and what works best for him.

Okay, so now you've found an object that your cat is interested in and will go after; getting Socks to bring it back to you is the next trick (and probably the "trickiest" part!). As with all tricks and training techniques, you have to know what motivates the particular cat you're working with so that you can entice and reward him appropriately. If Socks is strictly motivated by food-related treats, lucky you! Food is the easiest tool with which to teach your cat that if he fetches an object and returns it to you, he will receive something he desires.

Encourage repeat performances by practicing proper pet etiquette. Keep the following "feline manners" in mind:

- Reward Socks each and every time he fetches.

- Never tease Socks by sometimes giving him a treat and sometimes not. (Remember, cats are *not* dogs and they do *not* easily fall for treachery—nor do they easily forgive.)

- Be careful, though, not to overdo it on the treats—you don't want your fit feline to become a fat feline!

as a last resort

If you have a cat who does not respond to the "trick-and-treat" method, the other reward you can give is praise and petting. A lot of cats act as though they are above this kind of emotional bribery. Nonetheless, it does work on the many cats who don't realize they are performing a trick in order to get the attention that they so obviously deserve.

Once Socks figures out what's going on, he will be so used to fetching for you that it will be an enjoyable habit. As always, allow Socks to believe that retrieving is something he *wants* to do. In no time at all, you'll have your very own "golden" retriever—one dressed up in fine feline form!

hit the lights

One of my favorite late-night infomercials showcases those products that turn on the light by the mere clapping of hands. Our cats may be amused by our lack of night vision and even giggle a bit if our shins collide with the edge of a table as we grope in the darkness to reach for the light switch. With this trick, your agile feline can be a true friend indeed when you enter a darkened room. The beauty of this trick is that it is fun for your cat and gives her a chance to show off a bit.

pawing the spotlight

You must first teach your cat to paw an object or prop when instructed. The best introduction is to place your cat on a sturdy table so you can work with her more easily than at floor level. Put her in the "Sit" position (see chapter 2) about 12 to 15 inches from the edge of the table. Place a thick book (or other weighty object that won't tip over when touched at the edge of the table) between you and your cat. Hold a small food treat (use the premium type for this trick) in front of your cat. Make sure that the object is located between the food treat and your cat.

Say your cat's name and, "Paw," as you touch the object with the hand not holding a treat. As soon as your cat reaches for the food with one of her front paws and touches or steps on the object, say, "Paw, good, paw." Immediately give Fluffy a food treat and praise her.

If your cat is not touching the object, move it from side to side to entice her to swat at it. The instant she touches the object, say, "Paw, good, paw," and hand over the treat. This helps build the association between the object and the treat for your cat in training.

Repeat these steps about five or six times, or until your cat loses interest. Repeat these sessions daily. Be patient. It may take a week or more until your cat can perform the "Paw" command consistently.

let there be light . . .

Table training helps condition your cat to use her paw to touch objects on command. She has learned to perform this action while sitting on a surface above the ground. Now you're ready to put this groundwork training into practical use. Lights on!

Tap the nightstand in your bedroom next to your light switch. Shake a can of cat treats if necessary to garner your cat's attention. As you tap, say your cat's name and, "Up!" in an encouraging tone.

Once your cat is on the nightstand, pat the wall near the light switch and again give the "Up" command. Point to the switch and say, "Paw it." Help your cat flip the switch by gently guiding her paw. Deliver lots of praise each time she paws the wall in the right area. Practice this five or six times each session. Hand out plenty of treats.

Now, you're ready to add the "Lights On" command. Tap the wall near the light switch and say, "Up, lights on." When your cat presses the switch to turn on the light, praise and treat her. Repeat this command five or six times.

lights out!

What goes on, can go off. You can use these same basic hand signals to teach your cat the "Lights Off" command. Ideally, the best time to do this is when you are nestled under the comforter after reading a chapter or two from your favorite novel and are too lazy (or out of the way) to reach over and turn off the light. Call your cat by name, and say "Up, lights off." Shower her with praise before the two of you snuggle into sleepy time.

avoiding bedtime battles

Unless you are a self-proclaimed night owl, you probably use those hours when it is dark to get your recommended eight hours of sleep. This is the time of day when your body unwinds in peaceful slumber. Upon the rising of the sun, a new day begins and we—as people—wake up to face it. Unless, of course, something (or someone) has kept you up all night.

the 11 o'clock crazies

But if you are a cat, sundown means something entirely different. It's party time! Known as the "11 o'Clock Crazies" (or the "Evening Crazies"), this when cats decide it's the perfect time to get rowdy.

Cats are nocturnal. Just as many wild animals—including opossums, skunks, raccoons and bats—use the nighttime to explore and hunt, Fluffy uses it to play. Has Fluffy ever jumped on your head at 1 o'clock in the morning or attacked your defenseless toes at 3 o'clock in the morning? It's a very rude awakening and one that—with the correct training techniques—can be prevented. (Most of the time, anyway—an ornery cat may have an *occasional* slip-up.)

tuckering out your tabby

Getting your cat to go to bed when you do is actually not that difficult to teach. Since experts predict that the average cat sleeps 16 to 20 hours a day, getting Fluffy to go to sleep when you do shouldn't be *too* challenging as long as you can control her awake hours by spending time with her while you are home. Because cats have such short attention spans, the key is to stimulate Fluffy's interest right before *your* bedtime.

So when you get ready for bed, get out your cat's favorite toys and start some presleep playtime! You may even have to get down on all fours and chase Fluffy through the basement to make sure that she uses up plenty of feline energy. Believe it or not, Fluffy will tire herself out fairly quickly. Indeed, if you take the following steps you will soon be saying, "Goodnight, pussycat."

As long as your cat isn't on a special diet, give her a nightly can of her favorite wet canned food. This will do wonders for her sleep cycle.

routines are so (yawn) tiring!

Most cats almost seem to *need* a routine. So if you can establish a nightly routine of playtime followed by a tasty meal (think about how much you like to nap after a turkey dinner), your cat *should* be ready to settle in. But nothing is foolproof when it comes to felines.

zzzzzzzzzzzzzzz . . .

A very hearty "Congratulations!" can be extended to you once you master this somewhat difficult trick. Now everyone in your household—people and kitties alike—can take a well-deserved catnap. Sleep well!

gimme five!

Cats can be quite handy—I mean, paw—minded. Some revel in tapping your leg when they want attention, especially when you're on the telephone or preparing dinner. It's your cat's way of communicating: "Hey, I'm down here. Stop what you're doing and pay attention to *me*." This trick will teach you how to convert—on command—that nuisance pawing into a real crowd pleaser. With practice and perfection, your cat may even outperform your dog. Well, maybe . . .

the paw slap

Cats are naturally front-paw oriented. You may be surprised at how easily you can train your cat to greet you like the cool cat that he is.

Select a quiet room and kneel or sit in front of your cat so that you are at the same eye level and within an arm's reach. Have your cat get into the "Sit" position (see chapter 2) and praise him.

Place a small treat, such as a piece of tuna or chicken (the smellier, the better), in your right hand. Let him sniff your hand to get him to focus on you and that prized morsel.

Touch your cat's left front paw with your right hand, still keeping a closed fist around the treat. Say your cat's name and, "Gimme five!" Gently guide your cat's left paw up with your left hand so that it touches your right hand. As soon as you touch, hand him the treat and congratulate him enthusiastically.

Repeat these steps a few times so your cat can get used to the verbal and physical cues. You want him to experience success.

Now you're ready to jazz up this paw shake. Put your right hand straight out, holding a small treat between your thumb and index finger. If necessary, touch your cat's left paw with the treat and say, "Gimme five," as you guide his paw upward. When his paw is at his eye level, touch his paw with the treat and say, "Gimme five." Give him the treat and bring on the praise.

Gradually put some more enthusiasm into your voice and your hand gesture so that the action becomes more of a sporty slap than a calm shake.

Repeat these steps a few times so that your cat learns to follow the treat with his eyes and understand that he reaps a tasty reward when he touches his paw to your fingers.

Limit each training session to no more than five minutes. You don't want your cat to lose interest before the session ends. Always strive to end the training when your cat performs the trick successfully.

mixing it up

Once your cat has *paw*-sitively aced this basic trick, he may be the perfect candidate for an advanced version of this trick.

Place your cat on a sturdy table and give him the "Sit" command. By selecting a table with a top at your waist level, you will be able to have more control over your cat. Hold the treat in your right hand and say, "Gimme left paw." Touch your hand to his left paw and reward him with the treat. Do this a few times to build up his confidence. Now hold a new treat in your right hand and say, "Gimme right paw," as you touch your hand to his right paw. Praise him and give him the treat.

Do a series of three or four "Gimme Left Paw" commands (treating each time). Be sure to accent the word "left." Then do a series of "Gimme Right Paw" commands, giving added oomph to the word "right."

If your cat gets confused by the right or left paw (something even some people are prone to do), say, "Oops, not yet," and wait to reward him until he offers the correct paw. Help him by guiding your treat-holding hand to the paw that needs to be raised.

Eventually, you will be able to have your cat perform this trick with pure praise, handing out treats intermittently.

take a stand

Sometimes it's difficult to differentiate between what comes *naturally* to a cat and what you can actually teach her to do with proper training techniques. Such is the case with this next trick—teaching Socks to sit up on her hind legs (like bears or prairie dogs do). There isn't anything cuter than seeing your four-footed friend standing on two legs in an almost human-like stance.

Sure, a cat will easily stand up to beg for something or to peek up over something if she can't quite see it when she's down on all fours. But some cats may never do this—or realize that they can—until you teach them the trick.

sitting pretty

Begin by placing your cat on a barstool or chair. Gently push her hind end down so that she is in the sitting position. Then, hold a treat or a toy up over her head and tell her in your trick-command voice, "Sit up!"

The first few times, Socks may automatically stand up and try to reach the item, but do not give it to her. Start over from square one: Gently press down on her hind quarters

so that she understands that you want her to sit. Of course, it is important to remember that, as with every trick, if your cat resists too vigorously, don't force the issue; you don't want your trick-teaching sessions to become something your cat will dread. To get your feline to perform tricks for you, she must be having fun and—with most cats—it's easiest to just go ahead and let her think that *you* are performing for her!

standing tall

After Socks is in the sitting position, hold the treat or toy a little bit over the top of her head so that she has to look up to see it. Once she spots her object of desire, tell her, "Sit up!" and she should reach for it with her paw—or paws. Each time, raise the treat a

little bit higher over her head until she is definitely standing up on her back legs alone. If she doesn't perform on the "Sit Up" command, take the object away and start over. Pretty soon, most felines are going to figure out exactly what they must do to get the treat or toy.

When Socks eventually *does* "Sit Up" on command, you can reward her with whatever tempting food item or fun toy you have been dangling over her head. Be sure to praise and pet your cat after she has performed this trick. Once Socks has learned to "Sit Up" and beg in her special place (the stool or chair you trained on), you may transfer her to the floor and repeat the process so that she learns to "Sit Up" on command—wherever she may be!

come & go as you please

here's a reality check: Indoor cats live longer than their outdoor counterparts. Outdoor cats live, on average, to age five. Cats kept indoors can live into their early 20s. You can, however, make your home a happy haven and safely bring a bit of the outdoors to your feline friend. The solution: a kitty door. This door opens into a safe enclosure that allows your cat to smell the fresh air, feel the breeze on his coat, cackle at tree-perching sparrows and catnap in the sunshine.

your automatic cat doorman

Our finicky friends can be quite indecisive at times. First, they howl at you to let them out the door. Then a few minutes later, they howl even louder for you to let them back in. Some cats seem to find some secret glee in this because they will do this in-and-out activity for hours if you let them.

Save time and your sanity by installing a free-access pet door that allows your cat to venture back and forth between the inside of your home and an outdoor pet enclosure. Say goodbye to your doorman duties!

the flap over cat doors

Select a cat door that matches your cat's size (slightly wider and taller than your cat). Consider the weather of your locale. A plastic flip door is adequate for mild climates but not for extremely cold or hot climates.

Your cat's very own feline-size door can be installed in any wooden door, in a wall, or in a screen door. You can install more than one door to the interior of your home, too, so that you can control your cat's access to different rooms at different times. Or you can provide a safe escape into a room where your dog isn't allowed.

Local pet-supply stores and catalogs offer a variety of pet doors; these doors' main feature is that they easily swing open when pushed by a cat's paw or head. Ideally, select a model that allows you to lock the door when you don't want your cat to venture into the outdoor enclosure.

step this way

Congratulations on your crafts-manship. The kitty door is open for business. Now comes the real challenge: How can you train your cat to use the kitty door?

When you are installing the kitty door and enclosure, encourage your cat to hang around and watch. Give him time to accept and understand the new addition to the home. Give him treats near the kitty door and locate playtime with his favorite toy near the kitty door so he associates this new door with good things.

Also spend some playtime in the outdoor enclosure with your cat so he knows that this is a safe *and* cool place to be.

Once the kitty door is in place, make it a new household rule to never let your cat in the house by any other route than through the cat door.

a grand exit

Select a quiet time to teach your cat the ins and outs of kitty doors. Choose a time when he won't be distracted by other sights or sounds. Sit on the floor next to the kitty door and call your cat by name.

Rattle the cat-treat canister or entice him with the aroma of canned tuna.

When your cat approaches you, slowly but firmly push open the cat door with your hand and call him by name. Place a treat right in front of the door and praise him as he gobbles it down. Then place a treat through the door to the other side. You may need to gently guide your cat through the door but praise, praise, praise him when he reaches the other side.

Open the door and show him a treat and beckon him to come back through the door to you. Once your cat seems confident entering and exiting with you holding the flap open, you're ready for him to perform solo. Stash a "can't resist" treat on the other side of the door for him to pursue. Once he is in the enclosure, hand over more treats so he learns that this new addition to the family's home is definitely the cat's meow.

cat's in the bag

Who knows where the expression, "Don't let the cat out of the bag," first originated. One thing is certain: If there is a paper bag lying on the floor, your cat will be drawn *to* it—and *into* it. Cats can't resist an open bag. Within seconds, they're inside, causing the bag to wiggle and jiggle like gelatin. But bag play doesn't have to be a solo act. Join in the fun to make this game twice as exciting for you *and* your cat.

safe "ground" rules

When you come home from the supermarket, you can easily fill your kitchen counter with bags full of food. If one of these emptied bags happens to drop to the floor in your rush to put food away, it immediately draws the attention of your cat.

Bags can be fun, but they can also be dangerous. Before you let your cat play, practice a few safety rules. First, never let your cat play with a plastic bag. She can swallow a piece of plastic and choke. She can also get tangled up inside and suffocate. Select only paper supermarket shopping bags. They are much safer! Grab a pair of scissors and cut the handles off to prevent them from catching your cat by the throat. And only use one bag so you can control the pace of the game. You don't want too many bags on the ground to overload your cat.

Establish yourself as the esteemed "Keeper of the Bags." In other words, decide when to let your cat in (and out of) the bag. Always store the bags out of paw's reach when you are not playing the game.

indoor "fishing"

Never underestimate the power of a brown bag. To your cat, it represents the ultimate opportunity to practice her hunting prowess and fishing skills.

Take your scissors and carefully cut a circle about the size of a tennis ball in the middle of the bottom of the bag. This should look like a wide peep-hole. Then attach one of your cat's favorite small toys, such as a furry mouse or a small plastic ball, to the end of a long shoelace or cotton cord 18 inches to 4 feet in length. Make sure to tie one end tightly around the toy so it does not slip off the string.

Place the brown bag on the floor on its side. To trigger your cat's interest, sprinkle a little catnip in front of the wide opening of the bag. Allow her

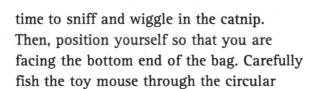

time to sniff and wiggle in the catnip. Then, position yourself so that you are facing the bottom end of the bag. Carefully fish the toy mouse through the circular

opening until it reaches about midway inside the bag.

Call your cat to the front of the bag.
Gently wiggle the toy mouse inside the bag
to grab your cat's attention. If she is like
most cats, she will raise her back end and do
a comical rear-end wiggle before diving
inside the bag to snare the mouse.

When she dives into the bag, quickly reel
the attached mouse out of the circular hole.
Your cat is left inside the bag, perhaps
extending a paw out
the peephole to
"fish" for the
elusive

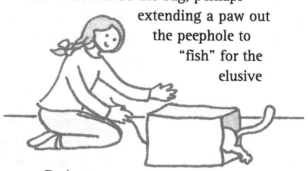

mouse. Praise your
cat for being such a terrific fisherman.
Give her a food treat.

Repeat these steps for five minutes.
Occasionally, allow your cat to capture the
mouse inside the bag and wrestle with it.
Spice up the game by attaching food treats
to the end of the shoelace, permitting your
cat to devour her "captured" prey.

Printed in the USA
CPSIA information can be obtained
at www.ICGtesting.com
JSHW012040140824
68134JS00033B/3168

9 781620 457269